STONEFISH

One stonefish sting can kill in minutes.

ZEBRA-FISH

Peacocks of the sea, zebra-fish are as deadly as they are beautiful.

SHARKS

Man-eating sharks include the tiger, mako, bull, hammerhead, and great white.

KING COBRA

The king cobra is the world's largest venomous snake.

SEA SNAKE

The sea snake is a big, ocean-going cobra.

DIAMONDBACK RATTLESNAKES

Diamondbacks are big, common, and American.

CROCODILIANS

Some big crocodiles include people in their diet. They'll swim miles for a good shipwreck.

VAMPIRE BATS

They aren't found in Transylvania; they live in the Americas.

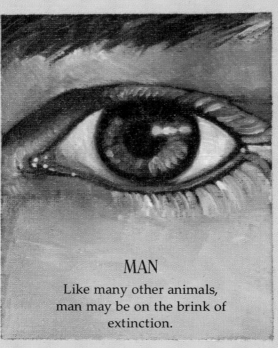

MAN

Like many other animals, man may be on the brink of extinction.

LIVING MONSTERS

THE WORLD'S MOST DANGEROUS ANIMALS

by Howard Tomb ♦ illustrated by Stephen Marchesi

SIMON AND SCHUSTER BOOKS FOR YOUNG READERS

Published by Simon & Schuster Inc.

New York • London • Toronto • Sydney • Tokyo • Singapore

SIMON AND SCHUSTER BOOKS FOR YOUNG READERS
Simon & Schuster Building, Rockefeller Center, 1230 Avenue of the Americas, New York, New York 10020.
Text copyright © 1990 by Howard Tomb. Illustrations copyright © 1990 by Stephen Marchesi. All rights
reserved including the right of reproduction in whole or in part in any form. SIMON AND SCHUSTER BOOKS
FOR YOUNG READERS is a trademark of Simon & Schuster Inc. Manufactured in the United States of
America.   10 9 8 7 6 5 4 3 2 1

Library of Congress Cataloging-in-Publication Data: Tomb, Howard, 1959-   Living monsters / by Howard
Tomb ; illustrated by Stephen Marchesi.   p.   cm.   Summary: Describes various dangerous animals, including
the blue-ringed octopus, scorpion, diamondback rattlesnake, and vampire bat.   ISBN 0-671-69017-5
1. Dangerous animals—Juvenile literature.   [1. Dangerous animals. 2. Animals.]   I. Marchesi, Stephen, ill.
II. Title.   QL100.T66   1990   591.6'5—dc20   89-28264   CIP   AC

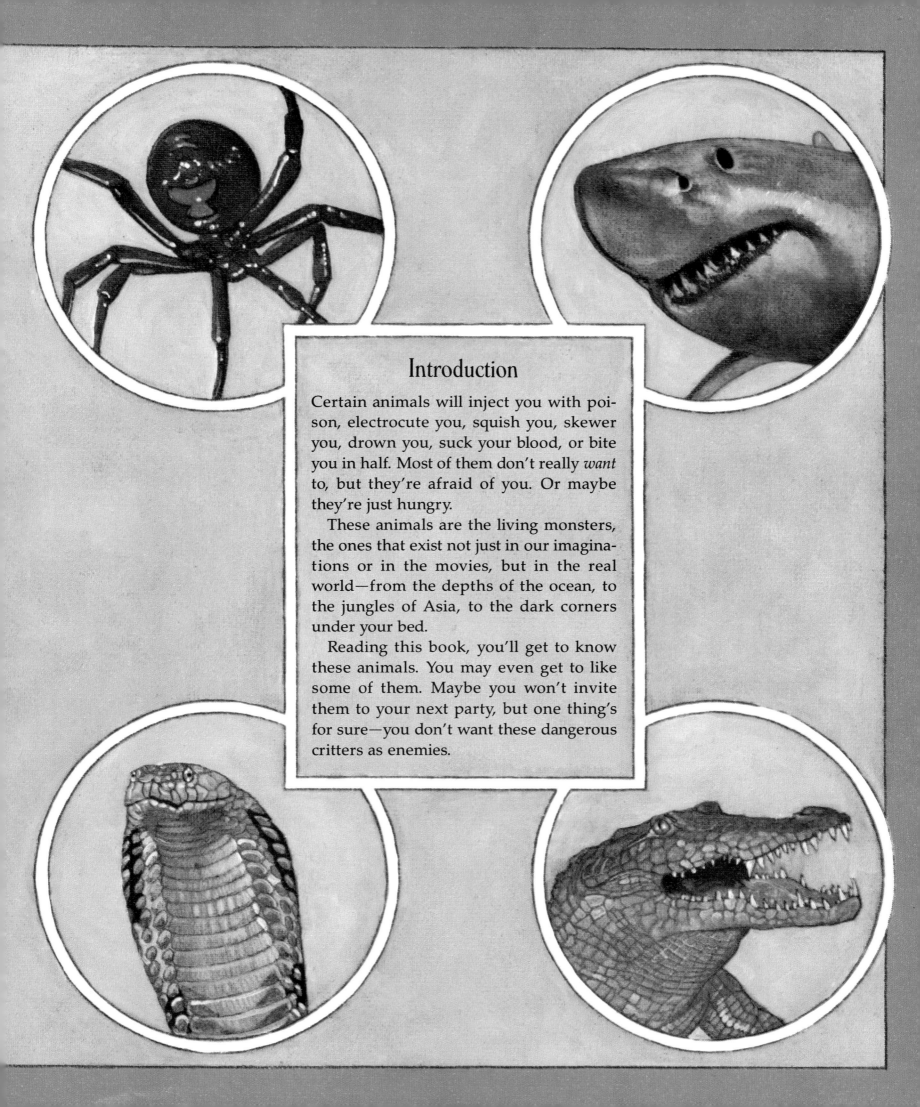

Introduction

Certain animals will inject you with poison, electrocute you, squish you, skewer you, drown you, suck your blood, or bite you in half. Most of them don't really *want* to, but they're afraid of you. Or maybe they're just hungry.

These animals are the living monsters, the ones that exist not just in our imaginations or in the movies, but in the real world—from the depths of the ocean, to the jungles of Asia, to the dark corners under your bed.

Reading this book, you'll get to know these animals. You may even get to like some of them. Maybe you won't invite them to your next party, but one thing's for sure—you don't want these dangerous critters as enemies.

SEA WASP

Jellyfish first appeared in the sea hundreds of millions of years ago, long before even the dinosaurs. With this head start, they have been able to develop some of the deadliest weapons ever to appear on our planet. These are known as *nematocysts* (NEM-at-ah-sists), or "stinging cells," and they're so tiny they're invisible without a microscope.

At first, nobody knew what was killing people at beaches in the South Pacific. Swimmers would suddenly scream, leap out of the ocean, and die right on the beach. Some people died even though they were only ankle-deep in the water.

A common jellyfish like the Portuguese man-of-war was suspected, but nobody reported seeing its famous balloonlike body floating on the water where people had been stung. Scientists finally identified the culprit as the box jellyfish, also known as the "sea wasp."

The sea wasp has tens of millions of stinging cells in its wispy tentacles, which may be more than sixty feet long. The cells are packed so densely that over a hundred of them would be found in a place as small as the period at the end of this sentence.

Stinging with only one cell might cause pain, but the sea wasp stings with thousands at a time. One touch can kill a 200-pound man in less than ten minutes. The poison scrambles the commands issued by the victim's brain. As a result, the lungs stop breathing, and the heart stops beating.

Under a microscope, a stinging cell looks like a seed with a bump on one end. When the bump touches something, a tiny trapdoor opens, and a barbed hook springs out and sticks into the skin of the victim. Strong poisons flow out of the broken pod and into the wound made by the barb. Symptoms begin immediately.

The sea wasp doesn't have a brain, a heart, eyes, or even a mouth. It's really just a floating stomach with tentacles. Prey is digested in the "jelly" part of the jellyfish.

Besides "fishing," the sea wasp also uses its tiny weapons to defend itself, but why it has so many of them is a mystery. It could certainly kill fish for food and repel its enemies with fewer stinging cells. A jellyfish with millions of nematocysts is as dangerous as a monkey with a box of hand grenades.

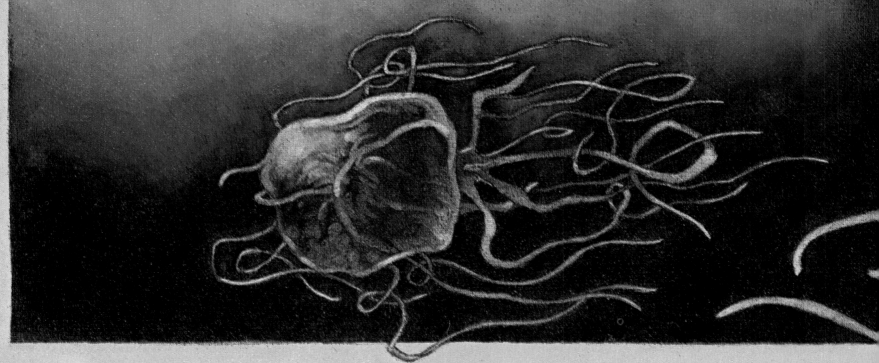

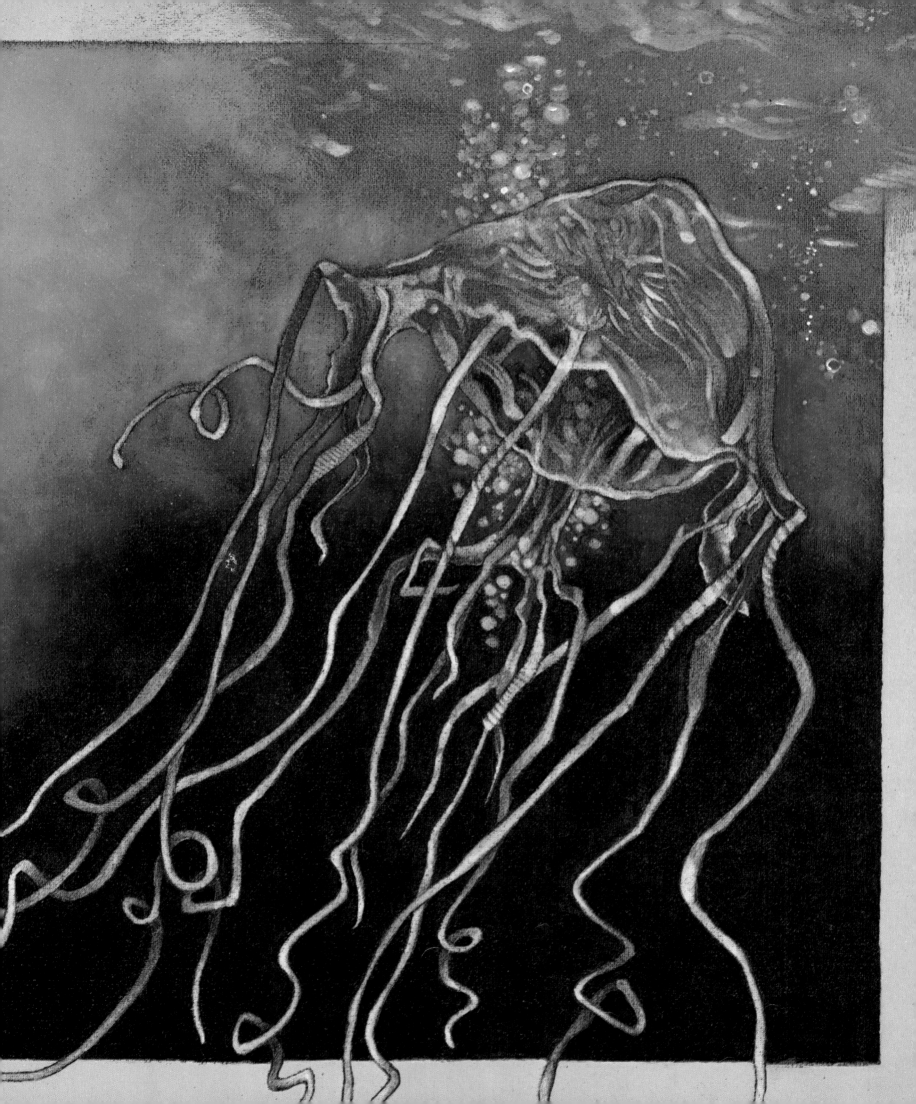

CONE SHELL MOLLUSK

How can a snail catch fish? With a poison-tipped harpoon, of course. Somehow cone shell snail "tongues" evolved into sets of barbed spears. That might seem like enough to allow the snail to hunt small fish. But the snail also developed a venom so strong it can kill a fish in a split second, or a person in a few minutes.

Even with a poisoned spear, hunting is still difficult, since every cone shell snail is completely blind. It locates prey by sucking water into its mouth and "tasting" it while hiding under the sand or near a rock. When a meal gets close enough, the snail slides a special fleshy tube toward the victim. At the last moment, the snail shoots or stabs the victim with one of the poisoned barbs that is inside the fleshy tube. The shot is so fast you can't even see it.

The snail holds each barb on a tough ligament, like a fishing line. If the prey tries to swim away, the cone shell snail remains firmly attached. If one spear is not enough, the snail may shoot several more. The poison begins digesting the victim from the inside out, like a rattlesnake's poison does to a rat.

There may be as many as 500 kinds of cone shell snails from Hawaii to Australia to the Seychelles in the Indian Ocean. They all have a similar shape, something like an ice-cream cone. The shells of adults may be as small as a grape or as big as a man's fist.

Cones have never attacked swimmers, but people do get stung because the animals live in shallow water and their shells are among the most beautiful in the world.

Some kinds are worth thousands of dollars to collectors.

The snails don't seem to like being picked up and may harpoon the curious beachcomber. Death may come in minutes.

It's easy to see why people who find cone shells on the beach can't resist them. But everybody should use a stick when investigating a shell on a tropical beach—the owner might be at home!

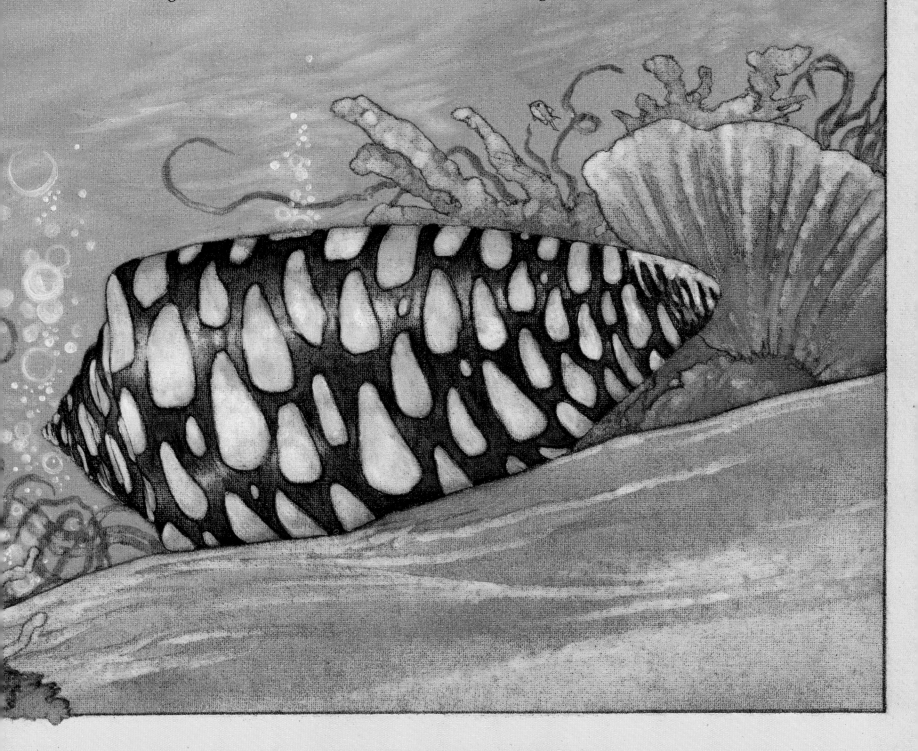

BLUE-RINGED OCTOPUS

Now and then, you see a giant octopus starring in a monster movie, but it's always made of rubber. In real life, big octopuses are shy and harmless. You're more likely to see them in a restaurant than wrapped around your leg. Besides, the biggest known octopuses weigh less than fifty-five pounds. The only deadly octopus is just a few inches long.

Where its eight arms meet its body, an octopus has a beak like a bird's. Octopuses use their beaks to kill and cut up their prey, and for self-defense.

The little blue-ringed octopus, however, does more than bite—it also spits into the wound. Its saliva is an extremely powerful poison. It causes *paralysis*, which means the victim can't move. This is perfect for the octopus—it can then either eat its prey or escape from danger.

Dozens of people have died from the bite of the blue-ringed octopus, even though it is a rare animal. The exact number of deaths caused by the octopus isn't known, because the mollusk is found in the warm waters of the South Pacific, where many people live in small fishing villages far from hospitals and scientists.

If people who've been bitten can get to the hospital in time, doctors hook them up to machines to keep them breathing for a day or two until the poison wears off. If the hospital is too far away, there is nothing that can be done. No *antidote*, or cure, for the venom is available. Even with medical attention, some bites are fatal.

The small size and beautiful colors of the blue-ringed octopus make it especially dangerous. When people see it in a tide pool along the beach, they may pick it up, not realizing how dangerous it is. When the mollusk is bothered, rings on its skin turn so blue they almost look electric. This is a sign that it's ready to bite; but to somebody who doesn't know better, it makes the octopus seem even prettier.

Most other octopuses are not poisonous, so they have to hide to avoid predators. They can change their colors in a split second to blend in with their background. But many dangerous animals, like the blue-ringed octopus, don't need to hide. Their enemies know enough to steer clear. The octopus's bright colors say to all the fish in the sea, "Here I am! Now back off!"

ARMY ANTS AND FIRE ANTS

Army ants are very small animals, but, pound for pound, they are the most terrifying predators on Earth.

A pound of army ants contains about 4,000 individuals. A 600-pound tiger is dangerous, but 600 pounds of army ants —2.4 million of them—could eat every speck of the tiger's flesh and leave only the skeleton, all in a matter of minutes.

Luckily for tigers, and for us, army ants hunt by the tens of thousands, not by the millions, and they can't march very fast. We are able to escape them by running away. Animals that can't run away are devoured alive. Army ants eat only living flesh.—never plants or dead animals.

Army ants, like many other kinds of ants, are blind. They can sense heat, which is one way they find prey. They also have a highly developed sense of smell, with which they detect all kinds of prey, including other ants. Army ants attack and destroy other ant colonies. Most ants defend their nest and their queen; but when army ants arrive, other ants won't fight—they abandon their posts and try to escape with their lives.

Army ants are fierce, warlike predators, and the warriors are all females. Male ants are created by the colony when they are needed for mating. They serve no other purpose—they don't go on the warpath with their soldier sisters, or even clean up around the nest. Male army ants can't get food on their own, and after mating, the females let them starve to death.

There are about five thousand kinds of ants, and they have developed all kinds of weapons since they appeared on Earth about 100 million years ago.

Only the female ant stings; her stinger is part of her reproductive organs. In addition to stinging, she may use it to bore through wood, probe the soil, and make scent marks. It is obviously useful, but its location at the tail end of the ant is troublesome. To sting, she has to stop walking and curl her tail beneath her. This is an awkward way to attack, so many ants have additional weapons.

Some ants bite and then spray a poisonous acid into the wound. They can shoot their poison up to 100 times their body length. For us that would be like spitting farther than a major league home run.

Other ants spray poison or glue in the face of an enemy, stunning it to allow the ants to escape or to give them time to attack it with bladelike *mandibles* (jaws).

Army ants live in the tropics. In North America, the most dangerous ant is the fire ant. It is very aggressive and attacks in large numbers, biting and stinging. While fire ant attacks are very painful to people, they are not usually fatal, because we can run away. But once in a while, people who are allergic do die from these ant stings.

Fire ants are actually used by people to attack other insects. The boll weevil is a terrible pest that eats cotton. Pesticides are not always effective in killing them, so farmers buy fire ant colonies, which are turned loose in cotton fields, where the ants feast on the boll weevils. It turns out that the best weapons against some insects are other insects.

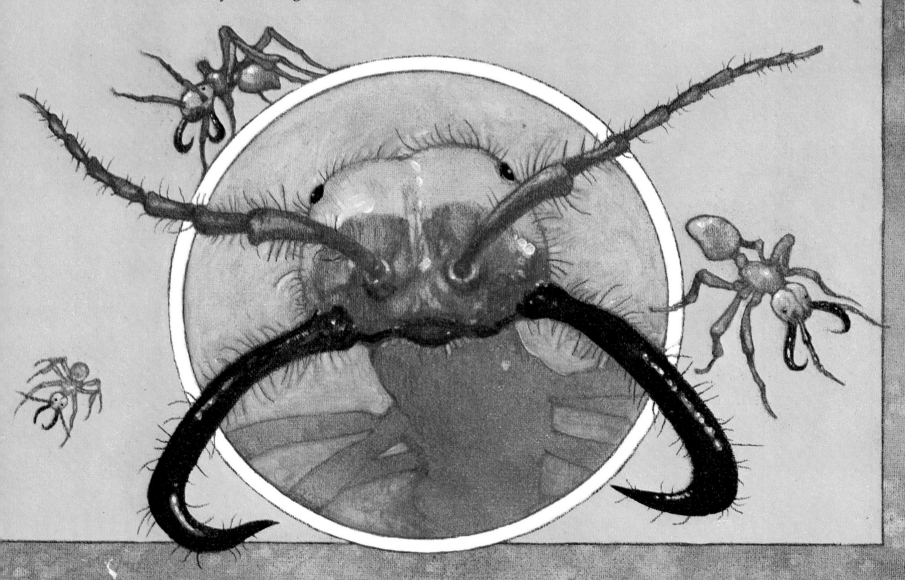

KILLER BEE

In the 1950's, dangerous African bees were brought to Brazil by beekeepers hoping to mate them with gentler European bees. But in 1956, the breeding experiments came to an end—one of the keepers mistakenly left the doors of the killer bee hives open, and the queens escaped, taking their thousands of loyal subjects with them.

Killer bees have the same kind of sting as other bees, and are about the same size. They're just more protective of their hive and their queen. If they sense a threat, they will attack in great numbers.

Our local bees—descended from European bees brought here by settlers—sting in smaller numbers. If you disturbed a nest of local bees, you would probably be stung no more than three or four times. If you disturbed a killer bee hive, however, you might be stung a hundred times or more.

Each bee sting injects a small amount of poison; and though some people are deathly allergic to even a tiny amount of this venom, most people get only a red, swollen spot for a day or two.

Killer bees got their name from the fact that when when they sting someone hundreds of times, they inject enough venom to be deadly.

Since they escaped, killer bees have killed hundreds of people in South and Central America. They've been making their way north for thirty years now, and are expected to begin arriving in the United States in 1989 or 1990. A welcoming party of scientists is waiting for them.

Killer bees don't make as much honey as their European cousins, so beekeepers are worried that the more aggressive killer bees will infiltrate local hives and hurt business.

Bees may also kill people who accidentally threaten the hives, perhaps by walking too close to them. Killer bees look pretty much the same as other bees, so special techniques have to be developed to identify and track them.

Military engineers have developed a tiny computer chip that has its own solar power station and laser transmitter. It's so small it can be glued onto a queen bee's body to track her movements. Scientists have invented another high-tech device—a killer bee detector, which can be worn on your belt. Flying killer bees sound slightly different from European bees. The detector picks up the sounds of nearby bees and gives a green light for "good" bees and a red light for killer bees.

In Asia, where other kinds of dangerous bees live, people have found a "low-tech" answer to their problem. They build shelters along roadsides and trails, where people can hide if they are attacked.

We have killed large numbers of the animals we thought were our enemies, from wolves to bears—some nearly to the point of extinction. But as far as we know, we have never come close to eliminating a species of insect. All we can do is monitor the insects and try to keep them under control.

SCORPION

The scorpion is a living fossil. It looks pretty much the same as its ancestors did 395 million years ago, before the dinosaurs appeared. Scorpions will probably be unchanged 100 million years from now, long after human beings have become extinct.

Scorpions are related to crabs and lobsters, and the resemblance is obvious. But after about fifty million years in the sea, scorpions came up on land, or became *terrestrial*.

In all that time, they've developed poison so deadly it can kill large animals like people. But scorpions are primitive in other ways. Their vision, for example, is poor, even though some have as many as twelve eyes.

They don't need good vision, though, because they hunt at night by feel. A scorpion walks along with its claws spread, and when they touch a bug, they snap shut. The scorpion then tears apart its victim and settles down for a meal. If it catches a larger or stronger animal, such as a tarantula, the scorpion may have to use its stinger to win the battle. The stinger is on the end of the curled tail, and the scorpion jabs it forward.

People often get stung by scorpions that have climbed into beds, clothing, or shoes. Scorpions come into houses looking for bugs to eat. They aren't picky about their food—scorpions eat each other, as well as black widow spiders.

The biggest scorpions can be eight inches long. (The pages in this book are nine inches wide.) These big guys are dangerous, but their smaller cousins are even worse.

The deadliest scorpions are small, only an inch or two long. They live in warm,

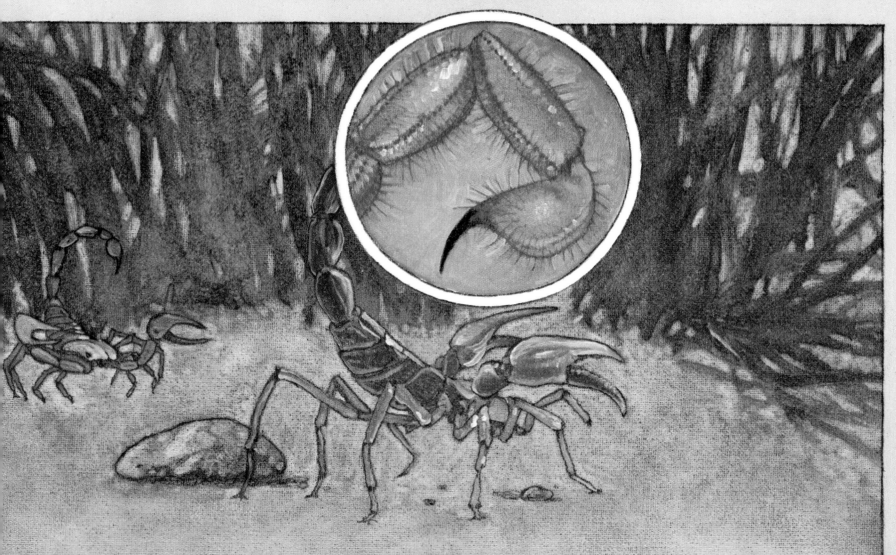

dry places in Central America, India, and Africa. A sting is painful, and the venom may act on the mind as well as the body. A victim may act crazy and even become violent. The person's hair may stand on end; he or she may sneeze repeatedly, grow numb, or throw up. Sometimes, a victim's eyes bulge and he or she goes blind.

Children get stung more often than adults, probably because adults know to check for scorpions when they put on shoes or get into bed. And because children are smaller, they are more likely to be seriously affected by the venom. In India, over half the children stung by one kind of scorpion are expected to die.

Like a snake bite, a scorpion sting can be fatal within minutes. But unlike snake venoms, scorpion venom has a special threat—it can kill even after a victim seems to have recovered from a sting.

Today, *antivenins*, the cures for scorpion stings, are made by scientists around the world. Still, no antivenin is perfect, and many people who are stung live a long way from a hospital.

In Mexico, scorpions kill more than a thousand people every year, so the government sponsors scorpion "roundups." A cash reward is offered for each one captured. One year, more than 100,000 were caught, but the problem didn't go away.

Scorpions are so small, so quiet, and so good at hiding that they can't be eliminated. After all, they were here more than 390 million years before we were, so they must be doing something right.

They have been very successful at adapting to different climates, and are found around the world in tropical areas, as far north as Oregon, and even in the Swiss Alps.

BLACK WIDOW AND BROWN RECLUSE SPIDERS

Scientists estimate that on an acre of typical farmland there may be more than two million spiders. With that many around, you might think they'd take over the world. But most spiders are tiny and harmless and eat only insects. Without spiders, *insects* might take over the world.

Spiders aren't insects—they're more closely related to lobsters and shrimp, which have eight legs, than to ants and flies, which have only six. Of the thirty thousand varieties of spiders discovered so far, only five or six kinds are dangerous to humans.

Most spiders are venomous, but they are so small that they can't hurt anyone. Some can't even break our skin with their bite. Their fangs are designed to kill insects, not people. But some spiders do have long enough fangs and powerful enough venom to kill a full-grown man.

Scientists disagree about which spider is the world's deadliest: the black widow or the brown recluse. These two are different from each other; but both live in the United States, and both are found in houses, where they can stay warm and dry. They started out in the tropics; but after people arrived on this continent, these little animals expanded their range, traveling with us in our cars, trucks, boats, and planes.

The black widow is smaller than a jelly bean, with a red hourglass shape on her back. The male, her mate, is pure white, and smaller than a grain of rice. He avoids his lovely wife except at mating time. She is about as romantic as she looks—she may eat him alive after they mate. They don't call her a widow for nothing.

The black widow is almost completely blind. Her web is not large and beautiful like a garden spider's. It's more of the "cobweb" type. She lives in the dark corners of closets, attics, basements, and garages, so good eyes wouldn't help her much. Her sense of touch tells her when prey is trapped in her web.

Spiders don't have jaws, so they can't chew; they can only suck. They either suck the blood out of their victims or inject digestive poison into the victim's body and suck out its innards after they turn to mush.

The black widow injects poison with her bite, and it hurts. In a few minutes, a

human victim may have cramps, and later may feel weak, become confused, throw up, or even become paralyzed. About one in twenty people bitten by a black widow dies. Survivors may feel sick for months.

Like the black widow, the brown recluse lives in the quiet, dark corners of houses, sheds, and woodpiles. It's also known as the "violin spider" or "fiddleback" because of the design on its back.

But brown recluse bites are different—they are often painless. About the size of a quarter, the brown recluse is bigger than the black widow, but you might not feel its bite for hours. First, you'd feel an itch like a mosquito bite, but it would get worse.

Eventually, you'd probably get a boil about the size of a half-dollar, and it might take months to heal. Doctors say that recluse bites remind them of bullet wounds. Today, special drugs can keep infections from getting started, so bites are rarely fatal.

The brown recluse can now be found in every one of the fifty states. It has a long life for a spider—up to three years. Unlike the black widow's husband, the male recluse is almost as big and dangerous as the female.

But in the race to be the world's most dangerous spider, the black widow may be winning. She and her relatives are found all over the world, from Australia to Argentina, from Iran to Indiana.

TICK

Spiders are scary, but when they bite us, they at least do so in self-defense. Ticks, which are related to spiders, bite us for dinner. They live on the blood of people and about a hundred other warm-blooded animals.

Ticks may be small, from about the size of a pinhead to about as big as a thumbtack. They live in grassy and wooded areas all over the world. They have powerful little jaws and, like spiders, eight legs.

A tick waits for an animal to brush against the bushes where it's waiting, and jumps on for a ride and a meal. When the tick finds a tender spot on the animal's skin, it digs its head under the skin to get to the blood.

Blood is too sticky for a tick to suck easily, so it injects some of its poisonous saliva to help the blood flow. Considering the small amounts injected by this tiny animal, the spit is very poisonous. It can cause paralysis and even death in people.

Luckily for us, tick paralysis is uncommon. But tick venom is not the only thing that makes ticks dangerous. Ticks also carry diseases that they may give to their victims.

Rocky Mountain spotted fever is carried by ticks in the western United States. Symptoms include a red rash, high fever and pulse rate, achy joints, fatigue, and, in some cases, death.

Lyme disease, another tick-borne illness, has been reported in forty-three states and seems to be spreading. The symptoms of Lyme disease are similar to those of spotted fever, with a few extras like mental and heart trouble, meningitis, and encephalitis. Both of these diseases are easy to treat with antibiotics if they are diagnosed early enough.

Chemical companies are developing pesticides and pesticide delivery systems to combat the ticks where they live. This is a tough fight. Ticks bury their eggs underground, beyond the reach of pesticides. They live on all kinds of animals, including mice, deer, and birds. Most pesticides are harmful to animals, and we don't want to kill the animals just to kill a few billion ticks.

Ticks will probably never be eliminated. The best way to protect ourselves is to wear long-sleeved shirts and long pants tucked into our socks when walking in fields and forests between May and July. Checking for ticks after walks can also help, because they may not bite for some time after hitching a ride.

One clever method of killing ticks is by sending mice home with fresh bedding. Cardboard tubes are filled with cotton balls that have been soaked in a special pesticide. The tubes are left outside where mice can find them. The mice take the cotton balls home to sleep on, and the pesticide kills the ticks carried by the mice, as well as fleas and lice, without hurting the mice.

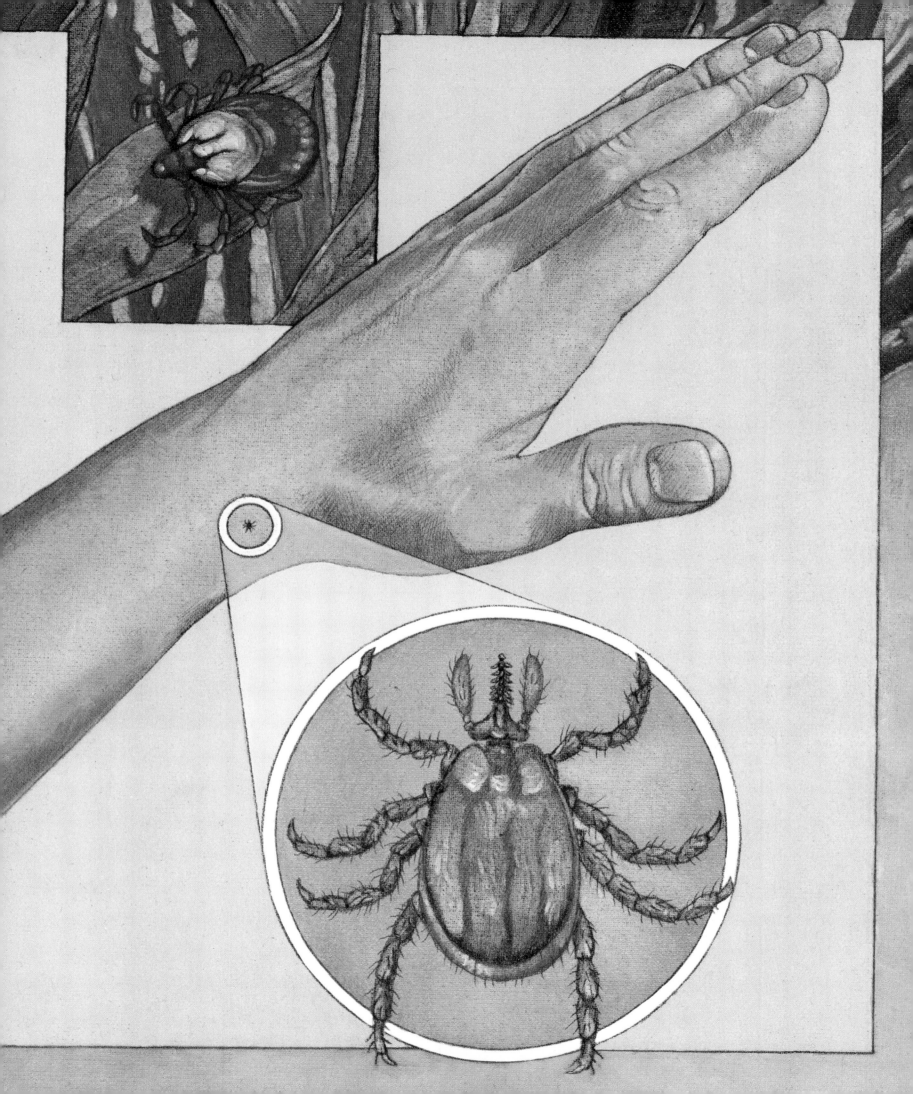

RAYS

To us, rays may look like aliens, but they've been here for hundreds of millions of years. We've been around for less than four million years. In their time here, rays have become a favorite food of many animals and have developed three ways to defend themselves.

Most rays are good at hiding. With their camouflage colors, they wiggle into sand or mud and lie still. Many rays have a powerful sting. Others are able to give an electric shock. Some can do all three: hide, sting, and shock. None of them can bite.

There are so many rays all over the world that they injure more people than all other fish combined. Some have even adapted to fresh water and are found in rivers such as the Amazon.

Many rays live in shallow water with a sandy bottom, the same kind of water we choose to swim in. A hidden ray is hard to see; and if stepped on, it will lash out with its powerful tail, driving its spear-like stinger into the unlucky wader. Careless fishermen are also stung when they pick up rays they catch.

A ray stinger would make a good spearhead. Legend has it that the ancient explorer Ulysses was killed by a spear made from a ray's stinger. Most stingers are four or five inches long, but a really big ray might have an eighteen-inch stinger (these pages are nine inches across, only half that size).

The stinger is so sharp it can cut through bone. Hundreds of barbs along the edges make a stinger hard to pull out if it breaks off in the wound.

You might think that the stinger by itself would be enough protection for a ray, but,

besides being sharp, each one is loaded with a poison that can be fatal. The wounds of survivors may be slow to heal. One Australian tough guy was stabbed in the leg and refused to see a doctor. His wound took *seven years* to heal.

Electric rays live in tropical oceans and rivers. They are also known as "numbfish" because after being shocked, your arm or leg might feel numb for a while. The shock probably wouldn't kill you.

Scientists think that an electric ray's shock might be used to stun fish for food. The ray's sting, however, is used only for self-defense, not for getting food.

Rays eat animals that live on the ocean floor, such as worms, shrimp, snails, and flatfish like flounders. A ray has up to forty-four rows of teeth, but these are for grinding food, not biting.

The enormous devil rays eat some of the world's smallest animals: *krill*. Some devil rays are more than twenty-five feet across and weigh close to 4,000 pounds, as much as a large car. A devil ray that size has a mouth three feet wide—plenty big enough to swallow a person.

But rays never eat people, and devil rays don't even sting. One of the most amazing moments in a sailor's life is when he or she sees one of these monsters "flying" out of the water and crashing back with a huge splash. Nobody knows why they jump.

Unlike some other fish, most rays don't lay eggs. Ray eggs hatch inside the mother's body, and the babies are born live. They are ready to sting at birth. How the mother avoids getting stung by her own babies is still a mystery.

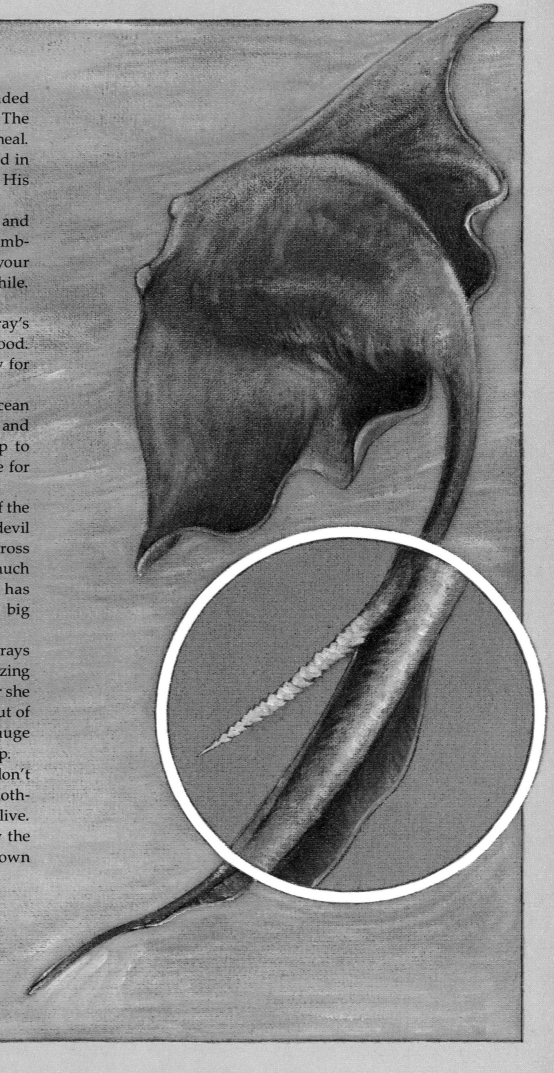

STONEFISH

A stonefish might be as small as your hand, or as big as a loaf of bread. Lying on the ocean bottom, covered with algae and partly buried, it's almost impossible to recognize.

Its slimy, warty-looking body has eighteen needle-sharp spines. Touching just one spine can kill a full-grown man in a few minutes. There may be enough venom in the spines of one fish to kill dozens of people. The sting is so painful that some people have tried to cut off their stung fingers and toes to stop the pain. Others have even tried to kill themselves.

You can see one reason why the stonefish has this name—it looks exactly like a rock. It also acts like a rock—it usually rests on the bottom in shallow waters and stays perfectly still. That's what makes it so dangerous. Unlike most fish, a stonefish won't move when a person is swimming or wading nearby.

The poisonous spines are not used to kill prey but only for self-defense. Nevertheless, the stonefish is one of the deadliest of the venomous fish in the sea.

Many poisonous animals, like some caterpillars and the stonefish's cousin, the zebra fish, have bright colors as a warning to enemies. But the stonefish needs camouflage to get food. It looks so much like a rock that even other fish are fooled.

Most fish prefer to stay near rocks rather than expose themselves in open water, so the stonefish lies perfectly still on the bottom and waits for a fish to swim by. When the victim gets close enough, the stonefish suddenly opens its huge mouth and the water rushes in, carrying the careless fish to its doom. Imagine how surprised a fish must be when it's swallowed by a rock it was trying to hide behind!

A bigger fish that tries to eat a stonefish is also in for a surprise. The poisonous spines on the stonefish's back are exposed, and sting the attacker.

As far as the stonefish is concerned, a person wading in the shallows is an enemy. Many people who are stung do not survive. Today, there are special drugs to ease the pain and antivenin to save a victim's life. But medical attention is not always available to victims in remote places.

Stonefish are very widespread. They are found in the Red Sea and in the Indian and Pacific oceans from Mozambique to the Philippines, where people swim and fish year-round. And because they can even survive being out of the water for several hours, they are sometimes stepped on by people walking on tidal flats.

ZEBRA FISH

To us, the stonefish is ugly and mean-looking, but its close relative, the zebra fish, is one of the most beautiful fish in the sea. Its wide-open eyes make it look more surprised than mean. It also goes by the name of "turkey fish" because its long spines look like turkey feathers and it sometimes "struts" underwater like a turkey.

Most zebra fish are less than a foot long. They live in shallow water but don't lie on the bottom like their cousins, the stonefish. Instead, groups of four or five zebra fish swim around slowly, looking lazy. They sometimes act curious when they see something unusual, like a scuba diver. They will swim right up and take a look.

Nothing seems to scare them very much. They never try to escape or hide. But if they are threatened, they may rush at their enemies and poke them with their spines. One touch may mean death for other fish and for people.

Everybody stays out of their way, and zebra fish use this to their advantage. They sometimes work together, forming a line with their fellow fish to "herd" minnows toward a zebra fish waiting to eat them. When one zebra fish has had its fill, it takes its turn herding so that other zebra fish can eat their minnow dinners.

Like the stonefish, the zebra fish has eighteen deadly spines; but people are not as likely to be stung accidentally, because the zebra fish is much easier to see in the water. The spines are grooved and covered with thin skin. When they touch something, the skin gets pushed back and the spines are exposed, allowing the poison to flow along the grooves into the wound.

People who are stung experience terrible pain and swelling. The poison affects all kinds of muscles, including the heart and lungs. When enough venom is injected, the heart and lungs will stop working altogether without quick medical attention. It's lucky for us that zebra fish are so easy to see and avoid.

Zebra fish can be found in warm ocean waters around the world, including the warmer waters of the United States and the Caribbean. Because zebra fish are so pretty, collectors keep them in aquariums as pets. But nobody tries to pet them.

SHARKS

Sharks will eat a lot of things. A captured tiger shark was found to have swallowed a keg of nails, along with a roll of tar paper and a carpenter's square. Nobody knows what happened to the carpenter, but the shark probably didn't eat him. Sharks don't seem to like the taste of people. The trouble for us is that we may not survive being "tasted" by a fifteen-foot tiger shark.

Sharks have special organs that allow them to pick up electrical signals. All living things give off small electrical signals, and sharks use these signals to find prey, such as animals in distress or fish hidden in the sand. Due to their electrical fields, metal objects like boat propellers may also attract sharks.

Sharks have been known to bite spinning propellers. Their bite is incredibly powerful, and their teeth are stronger than steel—so strong that they can actually bend and ruin the propellers they bite.

Sharks' relations with boats are not very good. They are very primitive animals in some ways, but they are among the smartest fish in the sea. Some sharks, when hooked, are smart enough to know that the boat has something to do with the hook. They may attack and even sink the boat.

Mako sharks are especially aggressive. They can jump as high as twenty feet out of the water, and have been known to jump *into* boats and attack the fishermen on board. Maybe the mako is trying to tell them they should stick to trout fishing.

The graceful tiger shark is even more dangerous than the mako because it will venture into shallow water, where people are swimming. Young tiger sharks have stripes. As they grow up, they lose their stripes and may reach eighteen feet in length. They kill more Australian swimmers than any other shark.

The bull shark is stout like the mako, and, like the tiger shark, the bull swims in shallow water. But bull sharks have a special ability—they can swim as far as 100 miles up rivers. Very few fish can go from salt water to fresh.

Bull sharks may be fourteen feet long; and because they are common and found all over the world, they are responsible for many attacks against people.

The hammerhead is the most unusual-looking shark and one of the most feared, not just by us but by other sharks, as well. Many sharks swim alone, but hammerheads swim in schools and include other sharks in their diet.

Nobody knows why hammerheads have their strange head shape, but it may allow them more "perspective" with their eyesight, hearing, and senses of smell, vibration, and electricity. Hammerheads may determine more accurately the direction of a fish in distress, blood in the water, or the sounds of a shipwreck.

Hammerhead sharks are truly fearsome animals and have been known to attack people. Some grow to be twenty feet long.

But no shark is more frightening than the great white. It is the world's biggest predatory animal, reaching a length of more than twenty-three feet.

Every year or so, a surfer gets bitten by a great white in northern California. Yet few of the victims are actually eaten. A great white may mistake a paddling surfer for a sea lion or elephant seal, two of its preferred foods. Unfortunately, its bite may be two feet across. Many victims don't survive the single bite they receive.

Northern California is popular with scuba divers as well as surfers, but great whites rarely attack divers. The sharks may be able to see that a diver looks nothing like a seal. Sharks are fairly intelligent, have fairly good eyesight, fairly good hearing, and a good sense of smell. Like crocodiles, they're pretty good at everything. That may be the secret of their success.

Sharks have been around for 300 million years, longer than the dinosaurs. The five sharks described here are all born live. Tiger shark mothers are pregnant for nine months, the same as people, and have only a few "pups" at a time. Sharks can't reproduce as fast as fish that lay thousands of eggs at once.

Some people, especially the Japanese, like to eat sharks, and kill them by the thousands. Shark fishing is also considered a sport by some Americans. Scientists worry that, without protection, these powerful, graceful predators may become very rare or even disappear. It might surprise a twenty-foot shark to learn that it needs our protection.

KING COBRA

The king cobra is the world's largest venomous snake by far. It grows to more than eighteen feet long—four feet longer than the average station wagon—and as big around as a man's leg. A coiled cobra that size can strike prey five feet away.

Not many things could be scarier than being bitten by one of these snakes. People who live in the king cobra's domain are so afraid of it that they may go into shock when they're bitten, even before the venom begins to take effect.

The poison injected by the king cobra's fangs is not as deadly, drop for drop, as that of some other snakes. The trouble is that the king cobra injects such large amounts of venom. Scientists say that one bite may deliver enough poison to kill more than a hundred people.

The king doesn't kill as many people as some other cobras do. The Indian cobra—the one with the yellow hood—is the one you most often see in movies. It lives mainly on rats, and because rats are *nocturnal*—they come out at night—so is the Indian cobra.

At night, an Indian cobra might slither around or even go into a house looking for a rat. As a result, people walking around in the dark get bitten. To make the problem worse, many Asians don't have shoes or boots to protect them from bites.

Unlike the Indian cobra, the king is not usually found around houses. It eats other snakes, not rats. It lives in remote areas from Thailand to the Philippines to China. The king is *diurnal*—it hunts during the day—so accidents with people are rare. It's easy to spot an eighteen-foot cobra in the daytime.

The people who are most often bitten are snake catchers and researchers who handle king cobras every day. In order to "milk" them, lab workers walk right into cages containing dozens of the deadly animals. In the lab, snakes are made to bite the edge of a glass or through a piece of rubber. This is known as *milking*. Venomous snakes of all kinds have their venom milked at laboratories and made into drugs and snakebite cures.

The king cobra could have earned its name because of its size alone, or because of the fact that it eats other snakes. But the king is also among the most advanced parents in the snake kingdom.

Most snakes leave their eggs after laying them, and the babies have to fend for themselves when they hatch. A king cobra mother is different; she makes a nest by coiling leaves and dirt into a pile. After she lays her eggs in the nest, she stays put to guard them. For a snake, she makes an especially good mother.

SEA SNAKE

Sea snakes are unusually shy. They bite only when threatened, which isn't very often. Few animals or people try to annoy nine-foot-long, oceangoing cobras.

The sea snakes' poison is meant for killing small prey and for self-defense. Sea snakes are big, but not big enough to eat people. They prefer fish and fish eggs.

Although swimmers almost never meet sea snakes, fishermen in Asia know sea snakes all too well. During their breeding season, the animals gather together by the millions. A fishing net may be hauled in containing more than a hundred of these deadly snakes, all struggling to escape.

Some grow to be more than nine feet long and get to be as big around as the fat part of a baseball bat.

The fishermen must throw the snakes back into the ocean, one by one. Of course, this kind of thing upsets a snake, and it may try to bite. Luckily, sea snakes have small teeth, so they have trouble biting through heavy gloves; but every year some fishermen have bad luck and get bitten.

The antidotes for certain kinds of sea snake bites are now available; but there are at least nineteen kinds of sea snakes known to have killed full-grown people, and antidotes are not available for all of their bites.

Sea snakes are descended from another deadly snake, the cobra that is found on land. Three or four million years ago, certain cobras took to the water. They may have been trying to escape their many enemies. Whatever their reasons, their move to the ocean was a good one—sea snakes have no enemies in the water.

Their move to the sea is almost complete. Today, many sea snakes can't survive on land. The others come up on dry land only to lay their eggs.

Sea snakes can hold their breath for up to eight hours. They may even sleep underwater while holding their breath.

They swim better than some fish, and can even swim backward. Special hatches, like a submarine's, seal their nostrils underwater.

Pacific Ocean fish will not try to eat a sea snake, even a dead one, although its flesh is not poisonous. In experiments conducted in the Atlantic, it was learned that sea snakes bit fish *from inside*, after being swallowed. The fish died in a few moments, and the snakes escaped right back out through the fish's mouths.

Sea snakes are found in coastal waters of the Indian and Pacific oceans, from South Africa to Australia to Mexico. If the snakes first went into the water in Asia, they must have traveled more than six thousand miles across the Pacific Ocean to reach Mexico.

There may be as many as fifty kinds of sea snakes in as many different colors. Some have black backs and bright yellow bellies. Others have bright blue stripes. Some are plain—a dull green or brown. But there is no trouble telling which ones are dangerous—they all are.

These oceangoing cobras have only one natural enemy: the eagle, whose feathers help it resist bites from the snakes' short fangs. There are also some people in Asia who like to eat sea snakes.

DIAMONDBACK RATTLESNAKES

Snakes can't chew their prey—their teeth are too sharp and pointy. But rattlesnakes have a way around this problem. Their venom is like the digestive juices in your stomach. When a rattler bites a rat, it dies in seconds. The snake then waits for a few minutes while the venom "digests" the rat's insides. When the victim's body gets squishy enough, the snake eats it whole, swallowing it headfirst.

The same kind of thing happens when a rattlesnake bites a person, but the poison isn't usually enough to be deadly. Instead, the bones and muscle near the bite are partly "digested," and when they heal, they may not work well anymore.

Rattlesnakes, like Indian cobras, eat rats and, like cobras, are often found around civilization. In suburban areas, where children play, rattlesnakes are considered to be more dangerous than rats. Although rattlers in populated areas are often killed, they can be captured by trained snake catchers and moved to more remote areas.

The eastern diamondback can reach eight feet in length and weigh fifty pounds. Its cousin, the western diamondback, grows up to seven feet in length. They are the largest of the many varieties of rattlesnakes. Diamondbacks are found in fourteen southern states, from Florida to California.

Really big rattlers have enough venom to kill a person, but a smaller rattlesnake can be deadly only if its fangs happen to hit a major vein or artery. Luckily, that is rare, and today doctors can save most victims of rattlesnake bites.

Rattlesnakes are our homegrown snakes—they live only in the Americas. In the millions of years they've been here, they have been very successful in adapting to all kinds of conditions. They can be found from Canada to Brazil.

Before white people arrived with guns, millions of buffalo, elk, moose, deer, and antelope roamed North America. American snakes may have developed rattles to avoid being accidentally stepped on by these big, four-legged animals.

Loud and clear, the snake's rattle says, "Back off!" It is more a warning than a threat. Rattlesnakes know better than to bite big animals for food—even an eight-foot rattlesnake can't swallow anything bigger than a rabbit.

Some animals don't take the hint, though. They include animals that eat rattlers, such as hawks, eagles, and wildcats.

Some dogs and some people can't take the hint, either. They harass rattlesnakes or try to kill them. If all the rattlesnakes in an area are killed, rats and mice may get out of control.

If an eight-foot rattlesnake isn't frightening enough, imagine finding a den with a hundred squirming rattlers. In cooler parts of their range, rattlesnakes hibernate together in hollows or caves. When the weather warms up, they come out together for a breath of fresh air, and they are *hungry*. Look out!

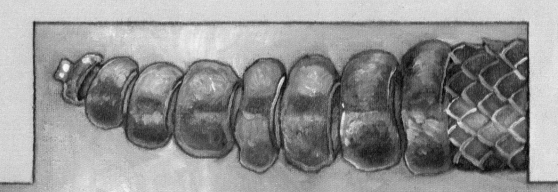

CROCODILIANS

Twenty-foot saltwater crocodiles have brains about the size of golf balls. You wouldn't think they'd be very smart, but these monsters have been known to hunt and kill in teams. Two crocodiles will grab opposite ends of their prey in their huge jaws and then roll in opposite directions, twisting their victim in half.

Crocodiles are among the most fearsome animals on Earth because to them, we are not frightening. We are dinner. But as scary as crocs are today, their ancestors were even more awesome. Ancient crocodiles grew to sixty feet, as long as a city bus. Their teeth were up to six inches long.

Crocodilians (crocodiles, alligators, and gharials) have been around for over 200 million years. Crocodilians, birds, and dinosaurs descended from the same animals; but the crocodilians and birds adapted and survived, while the dinosaurs did not.

Crocodiles and birds are distant relatives. Like birds, crocs and gators make nests, lay eggs, and take good care of their babies. The males and females work together and even call to each other, although they sound more like bulls than birds.

Birds have lost their teeth, but crocs haven't. Alligators have about eighty pointy teeth, crocodiles about seventy. These don't have sharp edges, like sharks' teeth. They are more like needles—they grasp prey so it can't get loose. When the teeth fall out, they grow back. In its lifetime, an alligator may have as many as 6,000 teeth.

When crocs and gators hunt a land animal, they lie motionless in the water, waiting for a meal to walk up to the shore. When they see one, they swim underwater toward their prey, storm up on shore, chomp onto the doomed animal, and drag

it back underwater to drown it. They also eat water animals, such as fish, frogs, turtles, ducks, and sometimes other crocs.

If the prey is small, a crocodilian will simply toss it back into its throat and swallow. But if the prey is too big to swallow in one bite, the croc has to tear off bite-sized chunks by twisting off parts. Sometimes that is difficult, especially if there's no team member to hold onto the other end. In that case, a croc or gator pushes the prey beneath an underwater log to let it rot for a few days, until it is soft enough to tear apart.

They live in warm salt and fresh waters all over the world. The largest and most feared are saltwater crocodiles. They can grow to twenty-three feet and weigh about half a ton. A croc that big can swallow a man's leg in one gulp.

Many stories have been told about alligators in city sewers, and one is actually true. In 1935, a seven-footer was found in a New York City sewer. How it got there is anybody's guess, but it probably hadn't been there too long. In the right environment, an alligator will live to be ninety years old. A sewer, though, is not a healthy place for any animal. Even a monster needs clean water and a little sunshine once in a while.

The beautiful skin of crocodilians makes fashionable shoes, belts, luggage, and purses. Even though animals need their skin, people kill them for it. At least one species of alligator is already extinct because some people want to be stylish, no matter what the cost.

VAMPIRE BATS

There are more than a thousand kinds of bats, and they are among our best animal friends. One little brown bat can eat more than six hundred mosquitoes an hour, and one cave might contain as many as twenty *million* bats. Bats not only eat tons of insects, they also pollinate flowers.

Bats are so important to us that you might think people would like them; but some bats look fierce and scary, and most fly at night, so they are mysterious. Bats aren't flying mice—they're more closely related to moles, shrews, and hedgehogs.

Some people think bats get into our hair, but that isn't true, either. Bats navigate well and avoid hitting things like people, even on the darkest nights.

As bats fly, they squeak, whistle, and scream, usually at pitches too high for us to hear. They listen to their sounds bouncing off objects in the dark. This is called *sonar*, and is how bats find bugs to eat and avoid running into things.

Among twelve hundred species of bats, only three are dangerous to us—the three kinds of vampire bats. All three live in Central and South America. They usually drink cow blood; but they sometimes drink blood from other animals, such as birds, sheep, goats, pigs, monkeys—and people.

Vampires are soft and brown, about the size of hamsters, and have long thumbs, which they use like canes to help them walk. At night, they fly out of roosts in hollow trees, searching for sleeping animals. When prey is found, the bats land nearby and walk over. They are so quiet and their teeth are so sharp that they could bite your big toe and have a midnight snack without waking you up.

They make two tiny holes and begin feeding. A vampire bat can drink up to 40 percent of its body weight in blood; that would be like a man eating sixty pounds of food at one meal. Vampires are so small that they can't actually drain a victim's blood. They are dangerous because they carry a deadly disease—rabies.

Europeans may have brought rabies to the Americas by bringing infected dogs from home in the 1700's. The bats got rabies by drinking the blood of infected dogs, and spread it around by biting other animals.

Rabies is a terrible disease that sometimes causes its victims to go crazy before they die. Even the bats become crazy—they might fly around during the day, for example. Latin American cattle ranchers lose hundreds of cows during rabies epidemics. During a bad outbreak in the 1920's, on the island of Trinidad, eighty-nine people and thousands of cows died from rabies.

Killing vampire bats is difficult, because they often live with the "good" bats that eat insects and pollinate flowers. Killing off all the bats would be a disaster, so scientists have invented two ways that help reduce the rabies problem by killing only vampire bats.

Bats are caught in fine nets strung near their roosts. The backs of the vampires are painted, one by one, with poison. Upon their return home, bats grooming each other accidentally eat some of the poison and die. Also, cows can be injected with a chemical that doesn't hurt them but kills the bats that bite them.

It may seem cruel to kill bats for carrying a disease we brought to them, but so far scientists have found no other way to stop them from spreading rabies.

MAN

When we think of dangerous animals, sharp teeth and powerful venoms usually come to mind. We tend to forget about the world's deadliest creatures—human beings.

Sharks, for example, may be scary, but they kill only about thirty people in an average year. Snakes and scorpions are more dangerous; they kill several thousand people each year. But human beings are the most dangerous animals on Earth by far. We injure and kill hundreds of thousands of our own kind every year. And nobody has any idea how many millions of other animals we kill.

In the United States, rattlesnakes kill about 12 people a year. Meanwhile, there are over 20,000 murders, and drunk drivers kill 24,000 people. Americans killed 620,000 of their countrymen during the Civil War. In World War II, tens of millions of people were killed. Sea wasps kill 3 or 4 people each year.

Some of the chemicals we make are more dangerous than anything produced by other animals. House paints, pesticides, dry cleaning fluids, and hundreds of other modern products contain poisons that are sometimes accidentally or irresponsibly allowed to enter our air and water.

Not all chemicals are poisonous by accident. We make plutonium, for example, and use it in nuclear bombs. It is hundreds of times deadlier than the poisons of stonefish, black widows, or cobras.

We have built tens of thousands of nuclear bombs, and just one could flatten an entire city. These bombs are supposed to make us feel powerful and safe; but if they are ever used, we will all be in trouble. Everyone on the planet might die from the explosions and fires that would result, and from poisons released into the air. So much dust would be blown into the sky that the sun might be blocked out for months or even years. Nobody knows for sure, but *all life* could be wiped out right along with us.

A scientist looking at people for the first time might not see how dangerous we are. We don't have claws, our teeth aren't especially sharp, and our skin isn't even tough. What makes us so dangerous is something invisible—our intelligence.

Our intelligence allows us to communicate and plan, so we can work together to create powerful, complicated things like jet planes, computers, medicines, and countries. But as smart as we are, we sometimes misuse our special talents.

All of our intelligence will seem silly in the end if we ruin our planet. The animals that share the Earth with us may not be as smart as we are, but they aren't going to destroy it. So the next time somebody says something bad about an animal, remember which one is the most dangerous.

SEA WASP

The sea wasp jellyfish kills people who are only ankle-deep in the ocean.

CONE SHELL MOLLUSK

This mollusk is as beautiful as it is deadly. It has a flexible, needle-like proboscis with which it injects venom.

BLUE-RINGED OCTOPUS

The blue-ringed octopus is small, beautiful, and has a deadly bite.

ARMY ANTS AND FIRE ANTS

Pound for pound, ants are the most fearsome predators on earth.

KILLER BEE

Contrary to early predictions, killer bees have not become more docile during their journey to the United States.

SCORPION

On a warm night, American deserts can be thick with scorpions.

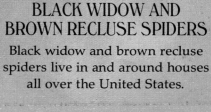

BLACK WIDOW AND BROWN RECLUSE SPIDERS

Black widow and brown recluse spiders live in and around houses all over the United States.

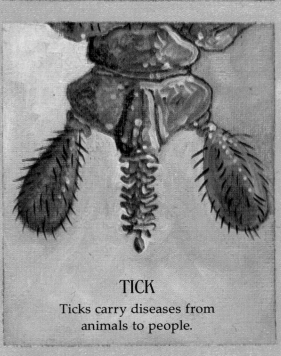

TICK

Ticks carry diseases from animals to people.

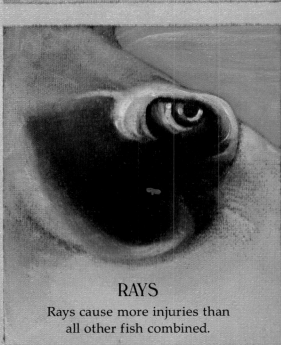

RAYS

Rays cause more injuries than all other fish combined.